# WHAT WE GET FROM CHINESE MYTHOLOGY

KATIE MARSICO

Published in the United States of America
by Cherry Lake Publishing
Ann Arbor, Michigan
www.cherrylakepublishing.com

Consultant: Jessica Anderson Turner; Marla Conn, ReadAbility, Inc.
Editorial direction and book production: Red Line Editorial

Photo Credits: Betto Rodrigues/Shutterstock Images, cover, 1; Fuyu Liu/Shutterstock Images, 5; Bildagentur Zoonar GmbH/Shutterstock Images, 7; Imaginechina/AP Images, 9; Edward Theodore Chalmers Werner, 11; Chan Chao/Thinkstock, 13; lzf/Shutterstock Images, 14; Babii Nadiia/Shutterstock Images, 17; Chris Gorgio/iStock/Thinkstock, 19; 123Nelson/Shutterstock Images, 21; Gordon Sinclair/Eye Ubiquitous/Corbis, 23; Imaginechina/Corbis, 25; Mary Evans/Ronald Grant/Everett Collection, 27; Lions Gate/Everett Collection, 28

Library of Congress Cataloging-in-Publication Data

Marsico, Katie.
  What we get from Chinese mythology / by Katie Marsico.
      pages cm -- (Mythology and culture)
  Includes index.
  ISBN 978-1-63188-911-0 (hardcover : alk. paper) -- ISBN 978-1-63188-927-1 (pbk. : alk. paper) -- ISBN 978-1-63188-943-1 (pdf) -- ISBN 978-1-63188-959-2 (hosted ebook)
  1.  Mythology, Chinese--Influence. 2.  Folklore--China--Influence.  I. Title.

  GR335.M375 2015
  398.20951--dc23

                    2014030284

Cherry Lake Publishing would like to acknowledge the work of
The Partnership for 21st Century Skills. Please visit www.p21.org
for more information.

Printed in the United States of America
Corporate Graphics
December 2014

## ABOUT THE AUTHOR

Katie Marsico has written more than 150 reference books for children and young adults. Before becoming a writer, Marsico worked as an editor in Chicago, Illinois. She lives in a suburb of Chicago with her husband and five children.

# TABLE OF CONTENTS

# A Land of Legends

Today, the People's Republic of China is known for its vast and diverse population. It is home to almost 1.4 billion citizens. They belong to more than 50 **ethnic** groups. They speak many languages, though the nation's official language is Mandarin.

China is filled with towering mountains and fertile farmland. It also has a long, fascinating history. From about 2100 BCE to 1912 CE, the nation was ruled by dynasties. A dynasty is made up of a series of rulers from the same family.

As with other cultures dating back to ancient times, the facts of China's history often blur with the region's complex, colorful **mythology**. Chinese **myths** often depict real-life **emperors** as gods. The emperors appear in legends alongside other gods and mythical creatures.

Some ancient Chinese storytellers used their tales to explain natural mysteries, such as how the world was

*China's dramatic landscapes have inspired myths for thousands of years.*

created. In other cases, they wanted to provide information about past dynasties. The stories of Chinese mythology feature many deities, or **divine** beings. In the myths, these gods and goddesses were responsible for shaping the universe. They controlled everything from weather to people's luck, both good and bad.

Chinese myths are also filled with a wide variety of incredible creatures. These include dragons, demons, and talking monkeys. Certain mythological characters are half-human and half-animal. Others use magic to shift their shapes. Their stories play out in a universe divided into heaven, Earth, and the underworld, or hell. In Chinese mythology, the land itself is alive. Spirits often make their presence known through nature.

Such beliefs were fueled by two major **philosophies**—Confucianism and Taoism. Confucius lived from 551 BCE to 479 BCE. He was a Chinese philosopher who advised people to work toward knowledge and self-improvement. He also encouraged

# LOOK AGAIN

*Look carefully at this picture. It shows one of the many fantastic creatures found in Chinese mythology. What do you notice about its appearance? Which animal does it most closely resemble?*

them to respect their elders and ancestors. The focus of Taoism is living simply and in harmony with nature.

A religion called Buddhism influenced Chinese mythology, too. Buddhists believe in reincarnation, or rebirth after death. They think a person's experiences and actions will affect his or her next life.

Evidence suggests that Chinese mythology existed as early as the twelfth century BCE. **Archaeologists** have found ancient oracle bones decorated with mythological images. Oracle bones are ox bones or pieces of turtle shell that were carved or painted with written symbols.

Myths were passed along through songs, dramatic performances, and storytelling. Some of the first written works about Chinese mythology date back to the fourth century BCE. Myths were often woven into collections of philosophical, religious, and historical texts.

Chinese mythology is rooted in ancient legends and tales, yet these myths have had a lasting **legacy**. Thousands of years after ancient people first created and

*Ancient Chinese people carved words and symbols into bones.*

shared their myths, Chinese mythology remains a collection of vibrant symbols from a remarkable culture.

# Amazing Myths

One of the most famous Chinese myths describes the creation of the world. This tale likely dates to the third century CE. It begins with a description of an egg-shaped cloud called the "cosmic egg." The cosmic egg holds the entire universe. At first, everything inside it swirls together in total disorder. Amidst this chaos, a giant god named Pangu develops. He sleeps and grows within the egg for 18,000 years.

At last, Pangu wakes up. As he stretches, the cosmic egg breaks. Some of the egg's contents float upward and

*In some myths, Nüwa has the body of a snake and the head of a person.*

create the sky and the heavens. Other parts drift down and form the earth.

According to another myth, the goddess Nüwa decided to create people after she felt lonely. She sculpted mud figures that resembled her own image. They came to life when she set them upon the soil. Nüwa used mud to populate the entire earth.

Human beings have important roles within Chinese mythology. Yet they are not the only characters with spirits and personalities. Many myths contain examples of animism. Animism is the belief that everything in nature is alive and has a **soul**. This includes rocks, trees, weather, and the land itself. Some types of animism suggest that, even after death, a person's spirit lives on in nature.

Animism influences how animals are portrayed in Chinese mythology. It is not unusual for animals to talk, experience emotions, or perform magic. Often, animal characters are turtles, monkeys, rats, pigs, and foxes. They frequently have fantastic features, such as multiple heads or human bodies. Some are even capable of changing shape.

This is a major theme in the folktale known as the Legend of the White Snake. The main character is a snake that uses magic to become a maiden named Bai Suzhen. She falls in love with a man called Xu Xian and marries him. Soon, though, drinking wine causes her to unexpectedly return to being a reptile.

*Dragons can often be seen in Chinese artwork, including sculptures.*

When Xu Xian learns of Bai Suzhen's true identity, he dies of shock. Fortunately, Bai Suzhen obtains a magical potion that brings him back to life. By the end of the story, Xu Xian realizes he still loves her. They become a family and have a son together.

Other myths feature dragons. In Chinese culture, these mythological beings are rarely portrayed as evil monsters. Instead, they are symbols of divinity, strength, and China itself. Dragons are also said to control water and weather. People in myths pray to dragons for help during droughts and floods.

Many stories from mythology reflect the real-life government and politics of ancient China. In the third century BCE, Emperor Qin Shi Huang ordered the burning of countless books. Qin Shi Huang wanted to rebuild the Chinese empire. He felt ideas from China's past threatened his vision for a new kingdom. Toward the end of the second century BCE, storytellers rewrote many of the myths that Qin Shi Huang had destroyed.

*Emperor Qin is famous for the more than 8,000 clay soldiers he ordered built to protect him in the afterlife.*

Many of these newer accounts featured a pantheon, or group of gods, organized much like China's imperial court.

In one myth, a Taoist god known as the Jade Emperor heads the pantheon. He controls the heavens, Earth, and the underworld. The role of the Jade Emperor is similar to that of actual imperial leaders. Lesser gods and spirits answer to him the same way lower-ranking officials once served China's rulers. For instance, the Kitchen God oversees the behavior of individual families. He then reports to the Jade Emperor, who uses this information to decide the families' fortunes.

## GO DEEPER

THINK ABOUT THE MAIN POINT OF THIS CHAPTER.
WHAT ARE THE MOST IMPORTANT DETAILS THIS CHAPTER
REVEALS ABOUT CHINESE MYTHOLOGY? FIND THREE
FACTS THAT SUPPORT THE MAIN POINT.

# LASTING LEGACIES

The legacy of Chinese mythology lives on in modern times. It influences everything from cultural celebrations to world-famous philosophies. For example, the creation myth of Pangu is an early example of the principle of yin and yang.

In Chinese philosophy, yin and yang are forces that make up everything in the universe. Yin is associated with darkness, cold, and negative energy. Yang represents brightness, heat, and positive energy. Despite being opposites, they combine to create an ideal balance.

*A symbol showing balance between light and dark is often used to represent the idea of yin and yang.*

In the myth, Pangu releases yin and yang when he cracks the cosmic egg. Yin is the heavier matter that floats to Earth. Yang is the lighter matter that forms the sky and heaven.

The idea of yin and yang is familiar to many modern cultures. It features heavily in Buddhist, Taoist, and Confucian philosophies. The popular symbol for yin and yang is a circle split into two teardrop-shaped halves. One half is white and the other is black. Each half contains a smaller circle of the opposite color. Today, this image is often used to show harmony.

The animism found in Chinese mythology has also left a cultural legacy. This is reflected in the Chinese zodiac. The zodiac is a chart with 12 sections that stand for periods in a 12-year cycle. The sections are represented by different animals. These are the rat, ox, tiger, rabbit, dragon, snake, horse, goat, monkey, rooster, dog, and pig.

A person's birth year determines his or her animal sign. In turn, the person is said to share certain qualities with that particular creature. For instance, a recent Year of the Goat lasted from February 1, 2003, to January 21, 2004. The zodiac predicts that people born during this period are likely to be loyal, good natured, and kind.

Various myths explain how the Chinese zodiac was created. One of the most popular myths involves the Jade Emperor organizing a race between animals. The participants had to swim across a fast-moving river.

## LOOK AGAIN

TAKE A LOOK AT THE CHINESE ZODIAC. WHICH ANIMAL SIGN ARE YOU?
GO ONLINE TO LEARN WHAT CHINESE MYTHOLOGY SUGGESTS
THIS SAYS ABOUT YOUR PERSONALITY.

The order in which the animals reached the shore reflects their placement in the zodiac.

These myths date to more than 2,000 years ago. Today, the zodiac remains a fascinating part of Chinese culture. Images of this chart often decorate menus and placemats in Chinese restaurants around the world.

Dragons have made a lasting cultural impact as well. Modern depictions of these mythological beasts are found in dragon boats and dragon dances. A dragon boat is a long, slim canoe. The front and back are designed to look like a Chinese dragon's head and tail. People all around the world race these boats during the yearly Dragon Boat Festival.

Chinese New Year is a popular time for dragon dances. A dragon dance involves a team of puppeteers supporting a huge dragon puppet on poles. According to many myths, performing the dragon dance is said to bring good luck.

Other holidays are also connected to Chinese mythology. The Jade Emperor's birthday is an important time within Chinese New Year celebrations. Offerings of food and burned **incense** are used to honor this divine ruler. People sing songs, light fireworks, and hold special ceremonies in Taoist temples. These activities are displays of gratitude to the Jade Emperor. People thank him for protecting them from evil, and they pray for his blessings in the year to come.

*Dragon dances often involve dragons that are more than 100 feet (30 m) long.*

# Art and Literature

Chinese mythology continues to shape art, language, and literature. Detailed ivory, porcelain, and **jade** carvings depict various gods and the animals of the Chinese zodiac. Ancient Chinese cultures viewed jade itself as a mystical "stone of heaven." It was a symbol of purity and other noble qualities.

Jade became a popular material for creating dragon sculptures. These creatures also appear in nine-dragon walls. Nine-dragon walls feature carvings of various dragons found throughout Chinese mythology. These

*Jade can be carved into amazingly detailed designs.*

walls exist in many places worldwide, from Beijing, China, to Mississauga, Canada.

Another reason Chinese mythology endures is because it appears in well-known works of literature. One of these is *The Investiture of the Gods.* Chinese author Xu Zhonglin wrote this novel in the mid-sixteenth century. It provides a fictional account of the creation of the Zhou dynasty. The Zhou ruled China from 1046 BCE to 256 BCE. *The Investiture of the Gods* involves several mythological characters, such as Nüwa, dragons, and fox spirits.

Mythology also plays a powerful role in *Journey to the West*. This novel by Chinese author and poet Wu Cheng'en was published in the late 1500s. It tells the story of a Buddhist monk named Xuanzang. Xuanzang must travel to India to retrieve sacred Buddhist writings. Along the way, he battles a variety of demons and monsters.

In *Journey to the West*, trees and animals, including scorpions and pythons, have spirits. Xuanzang's companions also include a monkey king and a creature that is half-pig and half-human. The Jade Emperor is referenced as well. *Journey to the West* has been translated and retold many times.

# LOOK AGAIN

LOOK AT THIS SCULPTURE OF THE JADE EMPEROR. HOW IS HE
DEPICTED? WHAT DO YOU NOTICE ABOUT HIS CLOTHING?

# MYTHOLOGY AND ENTERTAINMENT

Chinese mythology also lives on in the entertainment industry. In 1998, audiences flocked to see Disney's animated movie *Mulan*. *Mulan* is based on a Chinese legend about a fearless female warrior. This film also features a comedic dragon named Mushu.

The Legend of the White Snake has been retold for modern audiences, too. The story has been performed as an opera in China for decades. It served as the subject of a new, award-winning opera in 2010. The production, titled *Madame White Snake*, premiered in Boston, Massachusetts.

Martial-arts stars such Jet Li and Jackie Chan have helped spread Chinese mythology as well. In 2008, they

*The film* Mulan *features many aspects of Chinese mythology, including dragons.*

*The 2008 film* The Forbidden Kingdom *turns Chinese mythology into an exciting action movie.*

appeared in the film *The Forbidden Kingdom*. It contains some of the same themes and characters as *Journey to the West*. In July 2014, a cable television channel announced plans to produce a six-part series based loosely on *Journey to the West*.

References to mythological figures such as the Jade Emperor also appear in Japanese comics called manga. Other fantastic creatures from Chinese myths live on in video games. In the Super Mario series, the character Bowser is a dragon turtle. This mythological beast has a dragon's head and a turtle's body. Dragon turtles are also found in the game *World of Warcraft*. Meanwhile, the game *Smite* features the goddess Nüwa and characters from *Journey to the West*.

Many Chinese myths are rooted in ancient history, yet they have great appeal in the present as well. Storytellers will continue to enchant the world with the legacy of China's mythological stories and creatures.

## THINK ABOUT IT

WHY DO YOU THINK PEOPLE CONTINUE TO RETELL ANCIENT MYTHS? ARE YOU FAMILIAR WITH MYTHOLOGY FROM ANY OTHER CULTURES? HOW DO THESE STORIES COMPARE TO THE CHINESE MYTHS YOU JUST READ ABOUT?

# THINK ABOUT IT

- You have read how dragons are often portrayed in a positive light in Chinese mythology. Which other cultures mention these creatures in folklore and legends? How do their descriptions of dragons compare to the images created by Chinese storytellers?

- In Chapter Three, you learned that multiple myths explain the formation of the Chinese zodiac. Why do you think multiple versions of the same myth exist?

- Visit a reliable Web site or visit your local library to search for more examples of Chinese myths. Can you find more stories describing other mythological creatures? What about tales focusing on gods, magic, or human heroes? Do you notice any similarities between these myths and the ones mentioned in this book?

[ 21ST CENTURY SKILLS LIBRARY ]

# LEARN MORE

## FURTHER READING

Wang, Gabrielle, Sally Rippin, and Regine Abos. *The Race for the Chinese Zodiac.* Somerville, MA: Candlewick Press, 2014.

Yasuda, Anita, and Jok (illustrator). *Pangu Separates the Sky from the Earth: A Chinese Creation Myth.* Edina, MN: Magic Wagon, 2014.

## WEB SITES

**Asia Kids' Society—Stories**
http://kids.asiasociety.org/stories
Visit this Web site to read popular Chinese myths, including a selection of tales from *Journey to the West.*

**China-Family-Adventure—Chinese Culture . . . for Kids!**
http://www.china-family-adventure.com/chinese-culture.html#.U9cGKCwo74g
Explore this Web site for more information on dragons, the zodiac, and other examples of Chinese mythology and culture.

# GLOSSARY

**archaeologists (ark-kee-OL-uh-jists)** people who study ancient peoples through the objects those people have left behind

**divine (duh-VINE)** of, from, or like a god

**emperors (EM-puh-ruhrz)** rulers of a large kingdom or empire

**ethnic (ETH-nik)** relating to people that share similar customs, religious beliefs, or origins

**incense (IN-sentz)** a substance that is often used in religious ceremonies and that creates a strong smell when burned

**jade (JAYDE)** a hard gemstone often known for its green coloring

**legacy (LEG-uh-see)** something handed down from the past

**mythology (mih-THOL-uh-jee)** a collection of myths dealing with a culture's gods or heroes

**myths (MITHS)** stories that attempt to describe the origin of a people's customs or beliefs or to explain mysterious events

**philosophies (fuh-LAH-suh-feez)** particular sets of ideas about knowledge, truth, and life

**soul (SOLE)** the spiritual part of a person that, according to many religions, lives on forever

# INDEX